CHILDREN'S ESL CU

MW01223331

LEARNING ENGLISH WITH LAUGHTER

TEACHER'S GUIDE: BOOK 3B: ADVENTURES IN CANADA

Second Edition in Color

An Interactive Ready to Use Approach to Teaching English to Children.

This Series Includes a Student Book, Practice Book, and a Teacher's Guide with a Final Test.

The Children Will Listen to the Game Captions then Identify and Respond to the Corresponding Picture on their Game Card.

George and Daisy Stocker
Learning English with Laughter Ltd.
Victoria, B.C. Canada
V8X 3B6
E-mail: info@successfulesl.com

CHILDREN'S ESL CURRICULUM:

ISBN-13: 978-1500102395

ISBN-10: 1500102393

Published by:
Learning English with Laughter Ltd.
10 – 1030 Hulford Street
Victoria, B.C. Canada V8X 3B6
Visit us on the Web at:
ESL Curriculum: **http://www.successfulesl.ca**
Successful ESL: **http://www.esl-curriculum.ca**
English for Chinese: **http://www.englishforchinese.ca**
Printed in the USA

Customization of your covers

You may be interested in the customization of your covers. (White Label Services)
This personalizes your textbooks and makes them a visible part of your school's curriculum.
For this service contact us at: info@successfulesl.com

Members of our team with professional degrees have combined years of teaching experience and editing to produce these teaching materials.
Team Members for this publication:
Editors:
Daisy A. Stocker B.Ed., M.Ed.
Dr. George A. Stocker D.D.S.

CHILDREN'S ESL CURRICULUM:

A "LEARNING ENGLISH WITH LAUGHTER" PUBLICATION

TEACHER'S GUIDE BOOK 3B:
ADVENTURES IN CANADA

Second Edition in Color

Originally Copyrighted 2007
Second Edition Copyrighted 2013,
Learning English With Laughter Ltd.
10 – 1030 Hulford Street
Victoria, B.C. Canada V8X 3B6
website: http://www.esl-curriculum.ca

Learning English with Laughter Ltd.
Daisy A. Stocker B.Ed., M.Ed. and George Stocker D.D.S
1030 Hulford Street
Victoria, B.C., Canada, V8X 3B6
http://www.esl-curriculum.ca
e-mail: learning@efl-esl.com

CHILDREN'S ESL CURRICULUM:

TEACHER'S GUIDE BOOK 3B:

ADVENTURES IN CANADA

STUDENT BOOK

This sixth book of our Children's ESL Curriculum continuous series has an interest level appropriate for children 12 years of age and younger who are learning to understand, speak, read and write English as a second language.

It is assumed that they will have been introduced to the alphabet, beginning consonant sounds, and short vowel sounds. This book stresses the teaching of consonant blends. It introduces a new vocabulary of about 162 words that is built upon the vocabulary in earlier books in the series. Role-plays are an important part of this book. Pictures are provided throughout to facilitate understanding. Reading skills are developed by providing word repetition, phonics and dialogues. If the students are new to this series, the activities available in Guide Book 3A will help them to build the necessary speaking and reading vocabulary. The crossword puzzles reinforce the material that has been introduced.

The basic teacher instructions are given in small boxes on each page. It is important that the teacher repeat each question and guide the children's sentence answers. In this way the children are learning basic sentence structure and grammar.

TEACHER'S GUIDE

The colorful games provided in this Guide motivate learning. The children will always want to play again. The games also provide essential listening and speaking activities that build vocabulary and sentence structure. They are a very important part of the program.

PRACTICE BOOK

This book provides independent work for the children. The students will need a brief explanation of what they are to do before starting the pages that accompany each lesson.

Each student travels with the storybook characters and a classroom or an imaginary friend. This encourages imaginative ideas and stimulates student interest. The activities include drawing, printing, reading, printing question answers, role-plays and drawing their understanding of a situation. At this level sentence answers are shown in boxes. These provide the students with spelling, the correct verb tense needed to answer the questions and the word order of the sentences.

TEACHING PHILOSOPHY

This series is introducing English to young children as a second language where they are learning to understand, speak, read and write. As young children view their world as a whole, rather than in parts, an integrated approach is used. The activities include grammar, phonics, listening, saying or singing song verses, speaking through role-plays and printing. Graphics are used extensively to promote understanding, and are integrated with the speaking, reading and writing activities.

Note: You are the teacher – do it your way!
We wish you success with your classes,
Daisy Stocker B.Ed. M.Ed.   George Stocker D.D.S.
Learning English with Laughter Ltd.

CHILDREN'S ESL CURRICULUM:

TEACHER'S GUIDE 3B: ADVENTURES IN CANADA

CONTENTS:
(As presented in the Student Book)

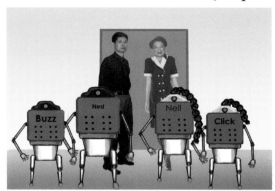

CHILDREN'S ESL CURRICULUM:

TEACHER'S GUIDE 3B   ADVENTURES IN CANADA

INDEX OF PHONICS AND GRAMMAR

(These page numbers refer to the Student Book)

BOOK 3B   TEACHER'S GUIDE
HOW TO PLAY PICTURE BINGO

Give each student one Bingo Card. For classes with more than 10 students, two or three students can have copies of the same card. It's best if those with identical cards are sitting apart.

The teacher calls the captions listed below in any order. The children are to mark the picture that matches the caption. For the first game they can all mark their picture with a small red **X**. When they have a horizontal, vertical or diagonal row of pictures with a red **X** in each box, they are to call **BINGO**. The diagonal row must go from corner to corner. The central BINGO box is free.
It is important that the children be allowed to help each other or be given teacher assistance. They should all find the correct picture to match the caption that is called. Although after playing two or three games they can be encouraged to work more independently, children should still be given help where needed.
The underlined words are new.

PRIZES: The winners will be delighted with a star drawn on their card or a rubberstamp picture.
The same BINGO card can be used for five or six games. To do this, have them use a different colored pencil for each game. For example, they might use red, then blue, then green and so on.
While playing this game, the children are highly motivated to learn by listening, understanding and associating the meaning to the picture. They are also learning basic grammar without any formal teaching.
This game will review some of the vocabulary used in the previous books of this series.
Play this game to introduce to Book 3B. The children will learn quickly if they play often.

BINGO 1 CAPTIONS (Call in any order.)   BINGO 1 ENRICHMENT CAPTIONS

BINGO 1 CAPTIONS (Call in any order.)	BINGO 1 ENRICHMENT CAPTIONS
This is Spencer's sister, Ruth.	Ruth is Spencer's sister.
This is Ruth's brother, Spencer.	Spencer is Ruth's brother.
Nell comes from Saturn.	Nell has a long braid.
This is a green jacket.	This jacket has a zipper.
This is Earth.	We live on Earth.
This is Saturn.	The planet Saturn has rings.
This is a robot dog store.	This store sells robot dogs.
Rockets go very fast.	The rocket has fire.
Buzz runs and claps.	Buzz runs fast.
This is a Whizzo chocolate bar.	The chocolate bar looks good.
Pancakes and bacon are good.	The pancakes are on a blue plate.
They run on the bridge.	A robot dog is on the bridge.
There's a present in the box.	The box has a ribbon.
The swing is under the tree.	The tree has a swing.
It's a loaf of bread.	The loaf of bread is long and brown.
It's nine o'clock.	The clock says nine o'clock.
The crab has ten legs.	The crab is in the water.
Spencer is wearing a T-shirt.	Spencer is wearing a red T-shirt.
Buzz can dance.	Buzz dances.
It's a sweater.	The green sweater has long sleeves.
It's a pair of socks.	These socks are red.
There's a star on Ned's stomach.	Ned has a red star.
Click has a cell phone.	Click talks on her cell phone.
Seals live beside the water.	The seal is on a rock.

This is Spencer's sister, Ruth.	This is Ruth's brother, Spencer.	Nell comes from Saturn.	This is a green jacket.	This is Earth.
This is Saturn.	This is a robot dog store.	Rockets go very fast.	Buzz runs and claps.	This is a Whizzo chocolate bar.
Pancakes and bacon are good.	They run on the bridge.	BINGO	There's a present in the box.	The swing is under the tree.
It's a loaf of bread.	It's 9 o'clock.	The crab has ten legs.	Spencer is wearing a T-shirt.	Buzz can dance.
It's a sweater.	It's a pair of socks.	There's a star on Ned's stomach.	Click has a cell phone.	Seals live beside the water.

BINGO 1   CARD 1

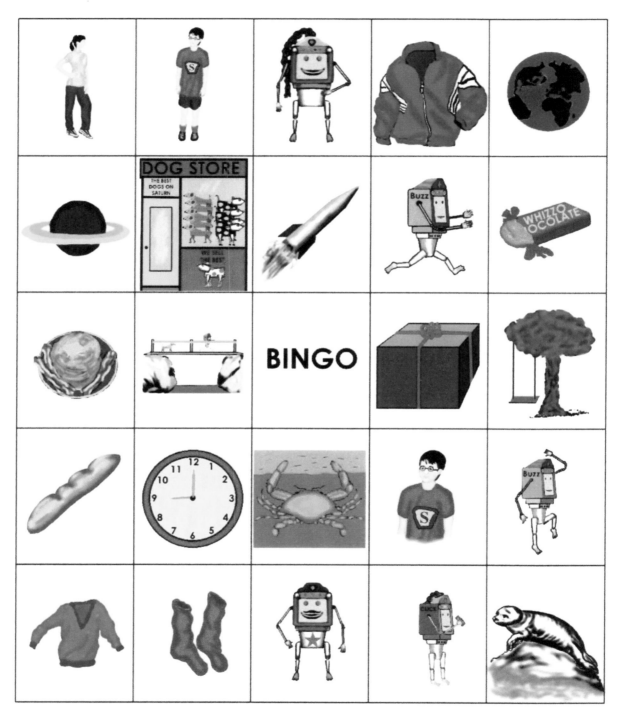

BOOK 3B   TEACHER'S GUIDE

BINGO 1   CARD 2

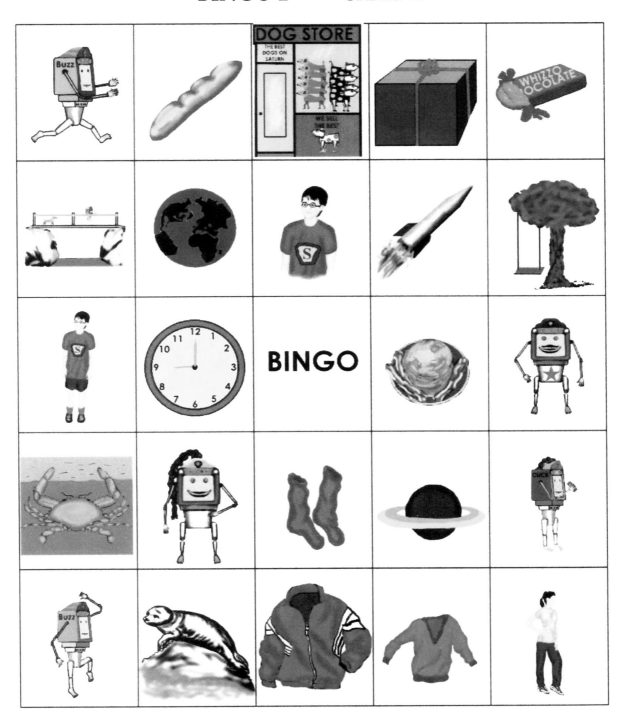

BINGO 1   CARD 3

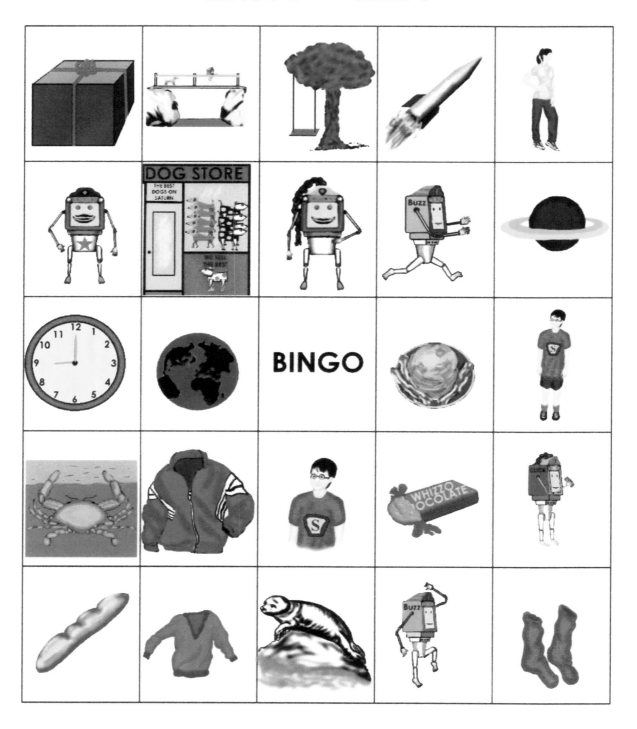

BINGO 1   CARD 4

BINGO 1   CARD 5

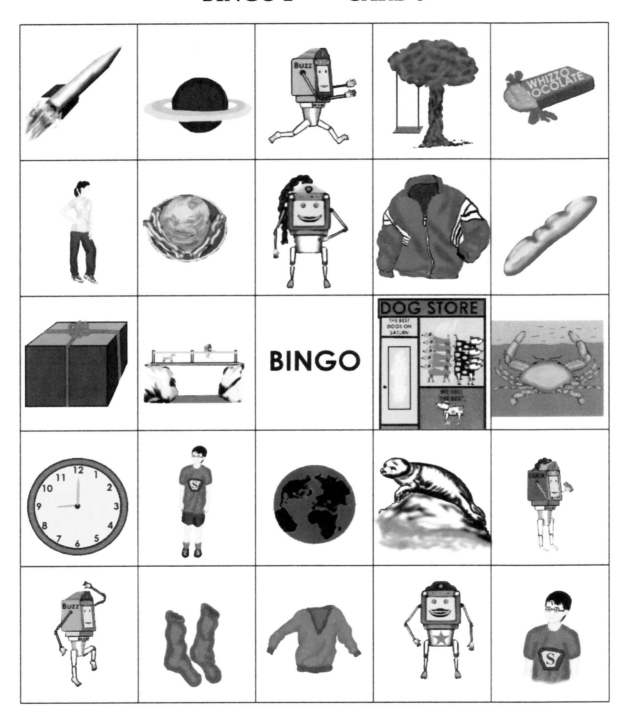

BINGO 1 CARD 6

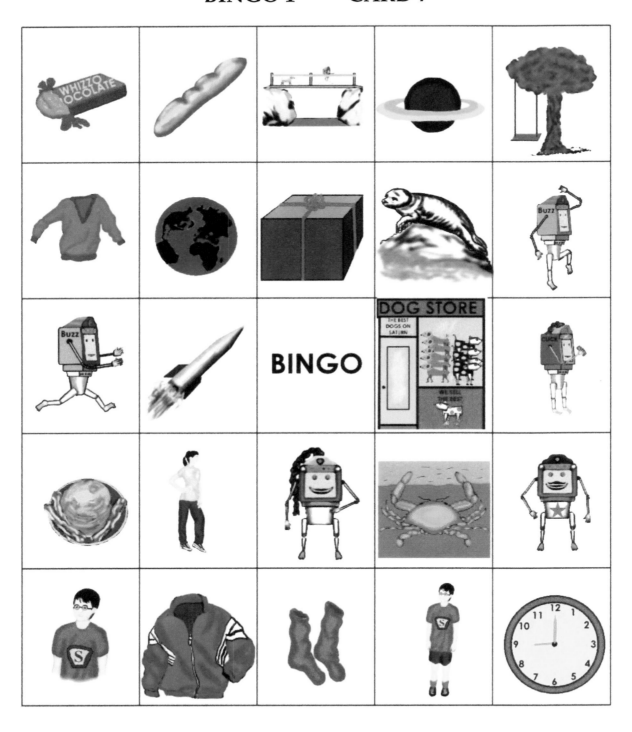

BOOK 3B　　TEACHER'S GUIDE

BINGO 1　　CARD 8

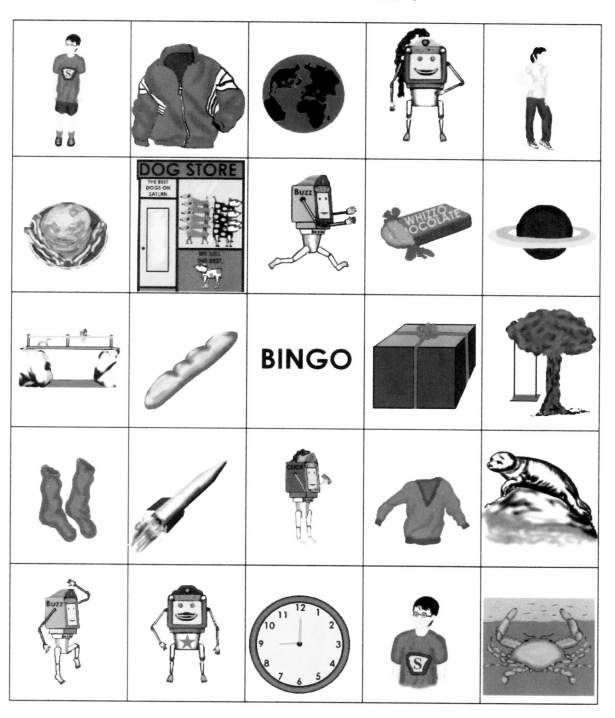

BINGO 1   CARD 9

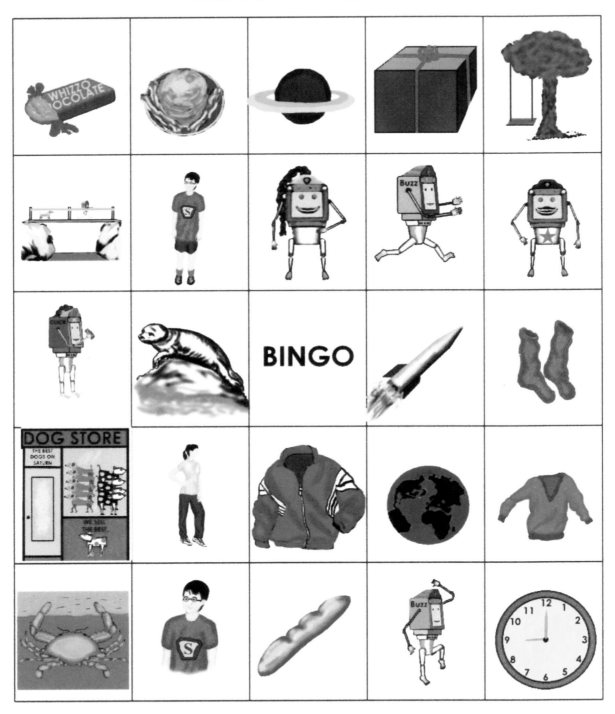

BOOK 3B   TEACHER'S GUIDE

BINGO 1   CARD 10

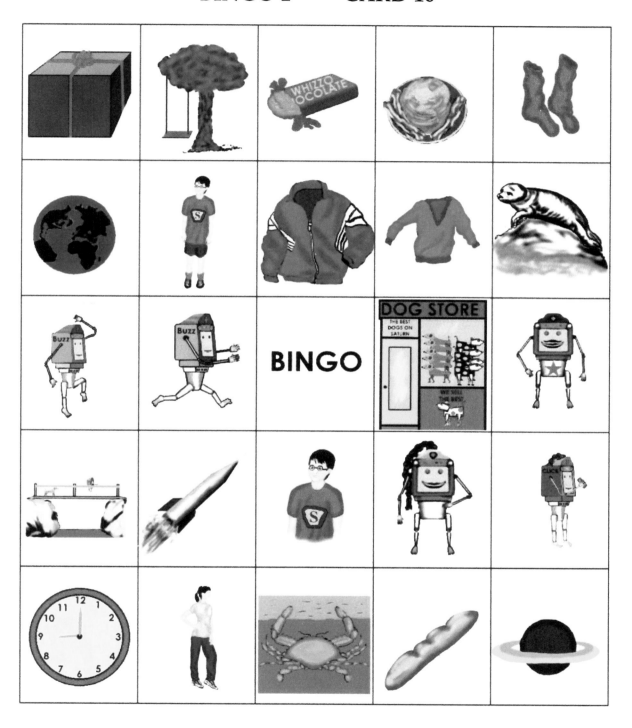

ANIMAL REVIEW

Use this activity near the beginning of Book 3B,
Adventures in Canada, after the first "Animal Review" activity.

Place the cards upsidedown on the table.

The students take turns picking up a card and naming the animal, insect, bird or reptile.

If they are right, they keep the card for the duration of the game.
If they make a mistake, they put the card at the bottom of the pile.

The student(s) with the most cards wins.

Prizes such as a stamp or a drawn star on a small piece of paper are very appropriate.
Sometimes the children like to have these put on the back of one of their books.

birds

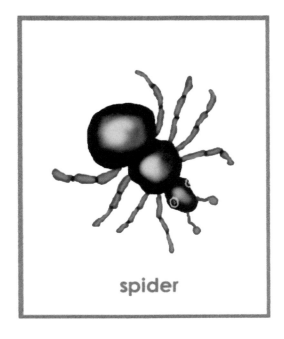

spider

monkey

tiger

panda bear

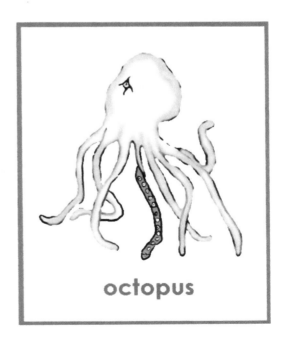

octopus

rooster

pony

turtle

rabbit

yak

zebra

woodpecker

alligator

dinosaur

dragon

fish

elephant

hippopotamus

goat

kangaroo

frog

lion

shark

giraffe

seal

BOOK 3B   TEACHER'S GUIDE

Crossword answers for Lesson 2, Page 7 of the Student's Book.

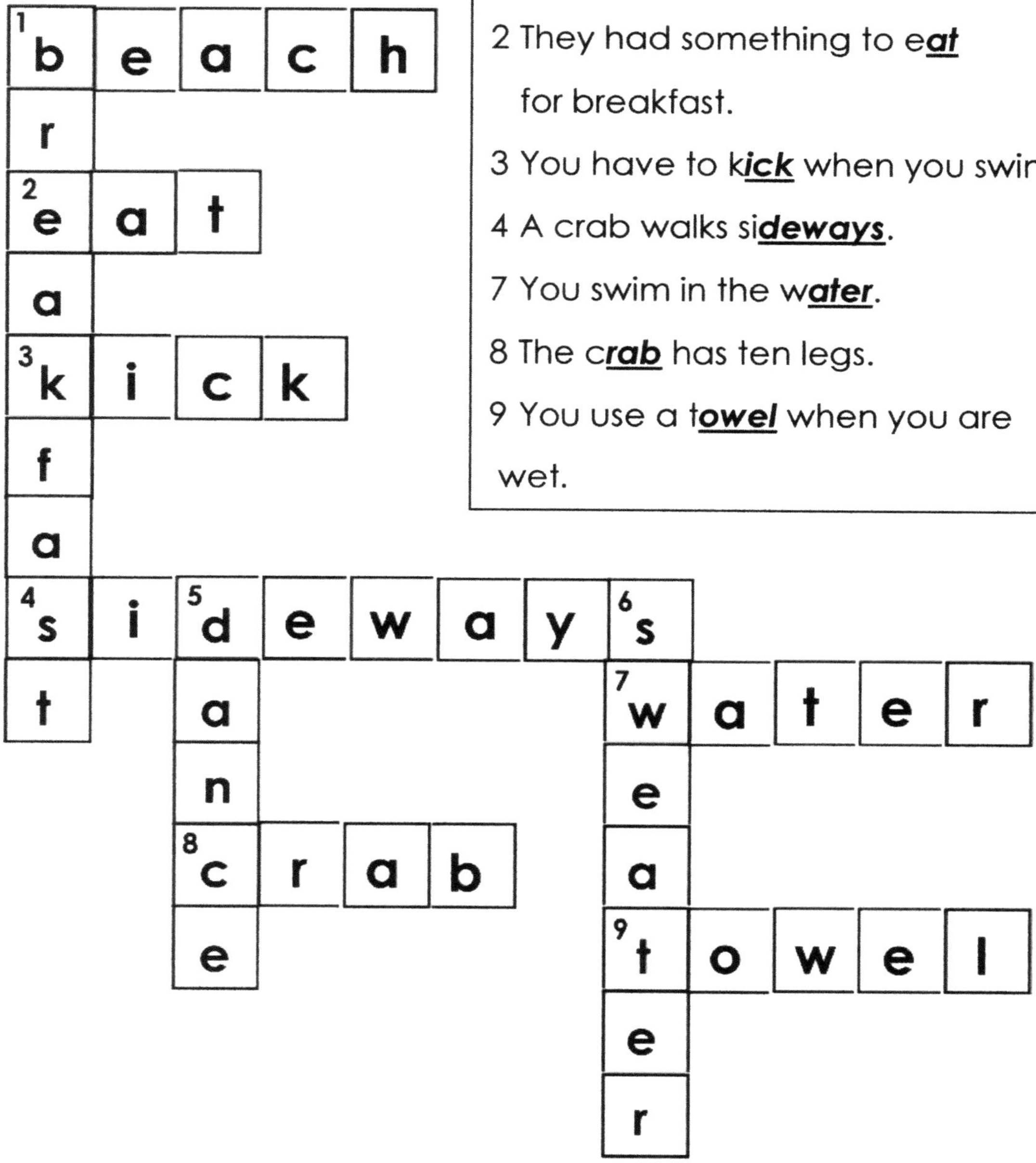

¹b	e	a	c	h
r				
²e	a	t		
a				
³k	i	c	k	
f				
a				

⁴s i ⁵d e w a y ⁶s

t a ⁷w a t e r

n e

⁸c r a b a

e ⁹t o w e l

e

r

ACROSS

1 The friends went to the b**each**.

2 They had something to e**at** for breakfast.

3 You have to k**ick** when you swim.

4 A crab walks si**deways**.

7 You swim in the w**ater**.

8 The c**rab** has ten legs.

9 You use a t**owel** when you are wet.

ANIMAL REVIEW 2
Use this activity near the beginning of Book 3B,
Adventures in Canada, after the first "Animal Review" activity.

This is similar to the earlier "Animal Review", but this time
the children must remember the name without reading.

Place the cards upsidedown on the table.

The students take turns picking up a card and naming the animal, insect, bird or reptile.

If they are right, they keep the card for the duration of the game.
If they make a mistake, they put the card at the bottom of the pile.

The student(s) with the most cards wins.

Prizes such as a stamp or a drawn star on a small piece of paper are very appropriate.
Sometimes the children like to have these put on the back of one of their books.

 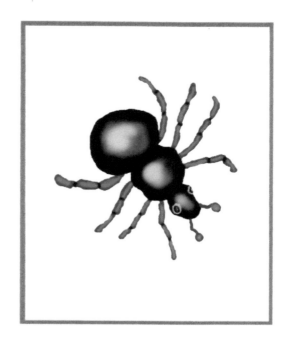

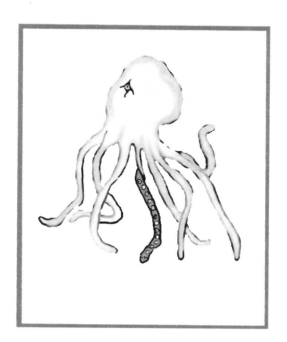

BOOK 3B   TEACHER'S GUIDE

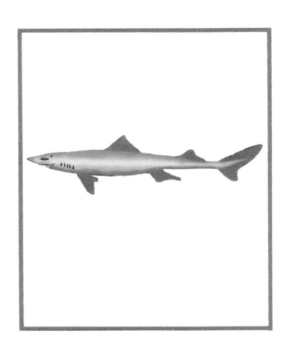

BOOK 3B   TEACHER'S GUIDE
PICTURE BINGO 2

For directions on how to play Picture Bingo go to Page 53 of this Guide.
These captions are also shown with their corresponding pictures on Pages 30 and 31.
Call them in a different order for each game.
The Enrichment Captions review the vocabulary that has been taught
and introduce some new words.
The new words are underlined on this page only.

This Bingo Game reviews the vocabulary taught in Lessons 1 top 5.

Bingo 2 Captions

There are four aliens.
The rocket is flying to Canada.
Buzz and Click dance.
Spencer is wearing his bathing suit.
The firecracker goes bang.
Crabs live in the salty ocean.
It's a crowd of people.
Nell swims with a life preserver.
Spencer is thinking about his flippers.
Ned floats on the water.
The water is up to Ruth's shoulders.
Click kicks when she swims.
Ned put both oars in the water.
Nell fell in the water.
They are fishing.
Ned has a towel.
The birds are above the water.
The plane is going up.
The fish is on the plate.
The chipmunk lives in the tree.
Saturn is far from Earth.
This is a fishing rod.
It's a pair of shoes.
It's a sweater.

Bingo 2 Enrichment Captions

The four aliens have square heads.
The rocket flies over the ocean.
The two aliens dance when they are happy.
He has a red bathing suit.
The firecracker makes smoke.
It has ten legs.
There are many people <u>together</u>.
Her life preserver is round.
Spencer could swim faster with flippers.
Ned spits out some salt water.
Ruth's head and shoulders are <u>above</u> water.
Click <u>splashes</u> and kicks in the water.
Ned is learning to row.
Nell fell out of the boat.
They have fishing rods.
Ned is drying <u>himself</u>.
The birds are flying over the water.
There are many windows in the plane.
The fish is on a pink plate.
The chipmunk jumps through the branches.
Saturn has many rings.
The fishing rod has a long <u>line</u>.
They are <u>running shoes</u>.
The sweater has long sleeves.

BOOK 3B   TEACHER'S GUIDE

BINGO 2   TEACHER'S COPY

There are four aliens.	The rocket is flying to Canada.	Buzz and Click dance.	Spencer is wearing his bathing suit.	The firecracker goes bang.
Crabs live in the salty ocean.	It's a crowd of people.	Nell swims with a life preserver.	Spencer is thinking about his flippers.	Ned floats on the water.
The water is up to Ruth's shoulders.	Click kicks when she swims.	BINGO	Ned put both oars in the water.	Nell fell in the water.
They are fishing.	Ned has a towel.	The birds are above the water.	The plane is going up.	The fish is on the plate.
The chipmunk lives in the tree.	Saturn is far from earth.	This is a fishing rod.	It's a pair of shoes.	It is a sweater.

The four aliens have square heads.	The rocket flies over the ocean.	The two aliens dance when they are happy.	He has a red bathing suit.	The firecracker makes smoke.
It has ten legs.	There are many people together.	Her life preserver is round.	Spencer could swim faster with flippers.	Ned spits out some salt water.
Ruth's head and shoulders are above water.	Click splashes and kicks in the water.	BINGO	Ned is learning to row.	Nell fell out of the boat.
They have fishing rods.	Ned is drying himself.	The birds are flying over the water.	There are many windows in the plane.	The fish is on a pink plate.
The chipmunk jumps through the branches.	Saturn has many rings.	The fishing rod has a long line.	They are running shoes.	The sweater has long sleeves.

=

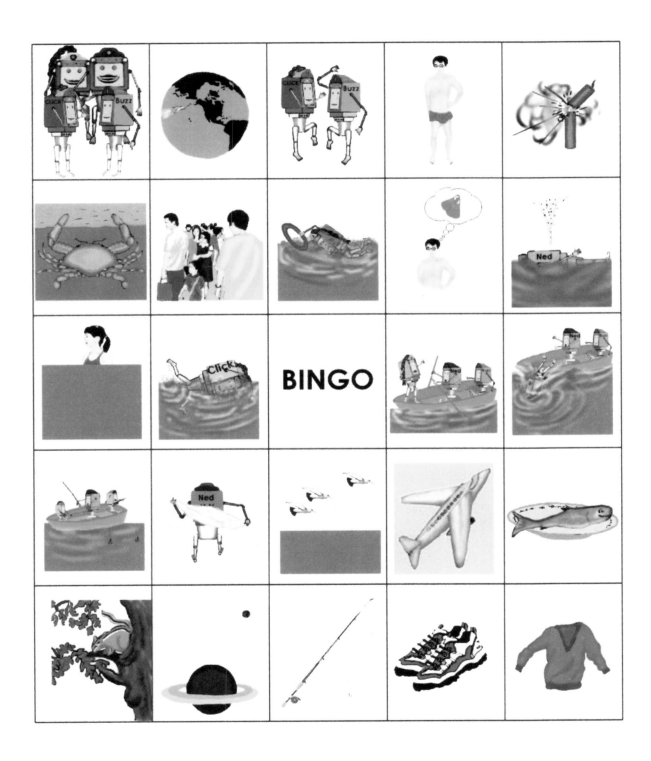

BOOK 3B   TEACHER'S GUIDE
BINGO 2   CARD 9

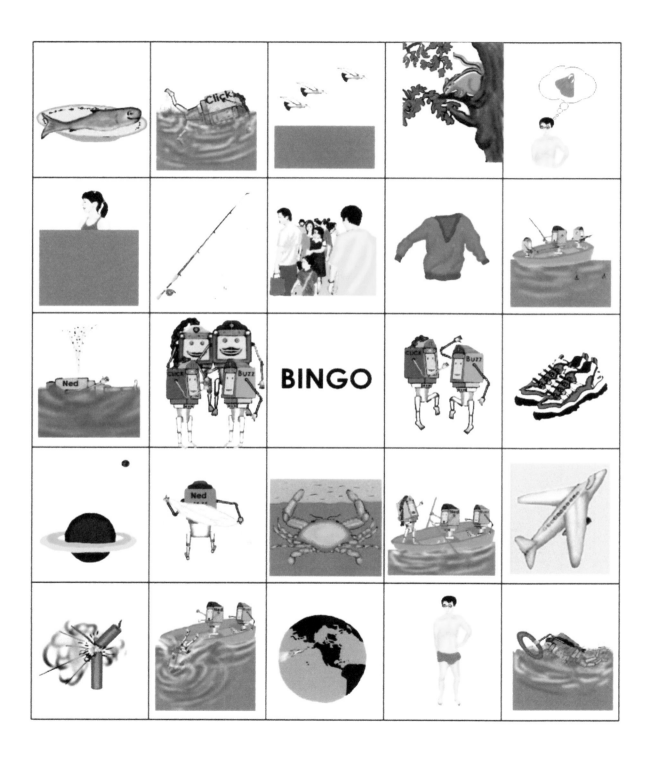

Answers to Page 66, Lesson 21

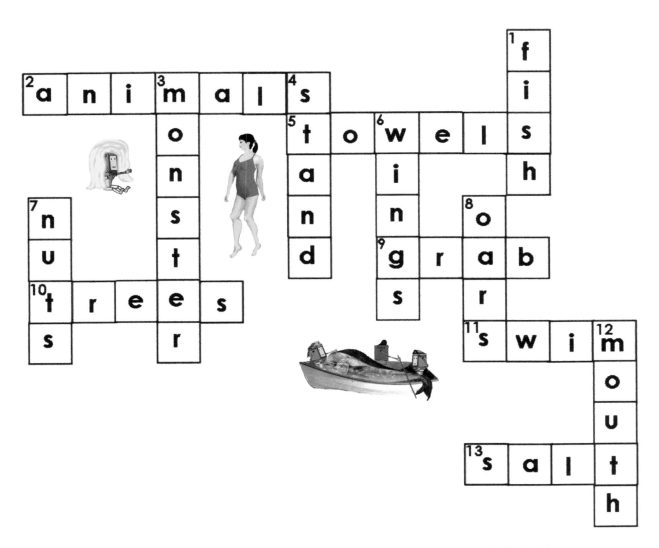

ACROSS

2   There are *animals* on the island.
5. They dried themselves with *towels*.
9   Nell had to *grab* the boat.
10 Chipmunks live in *trees*.
11. The aliens learned to *swim*.
13 Oceans have *salt* water.

DOWN

1   They caught a *fish*.
3   Click caught a *monster* fish.
4   Don't *stand* up in a boat.
6. Birds have *wings*.
8   They rowed with *oars*.
12 Ned got salt water in his *mouth*.

PICTURE BINGO 3

For directions on how to play Picture Bingo go to Page 53 of this Guide.
These captions are also shown with their corresponding pictures on Pages 96 and 97.
Call them in a different order for each game.
The Enrichment Captions review the vocabulary that has been taught
and introduces some new words.
These words are underlined on this page only.

This Bingo Game reviews the vocabulary taught in Lessons 6 to 9

NOTE: The pronoun "it" is used for animals and things.
"He" and "She" are used for people. (and aliens!)
In the enrichment captions the picture that refers to the whale says:
"**It** is swimming in the ocean."
Ned is floating in the ocean so the caption says:
"**He** spits the salt water out of his mouth when he floats."

It's an island in the ocean.
Ruth is rowing the boat.
It rhymes with sail.
It rhymes with near.
It's sitting on a branch.
It's a chicken.
It's a squirrel.
Click caught an enormous fish.
The boats are on the sand.
Click found a fish skeleton.
Spencer can make rocks skip on the water.
The birds have wings.
Buzz dries <u>himself</u> with a towel.
Ned got salt water in his mouth.
floats.
Ned smells something terrible.
Skunks are black and white animals.
Grandmother is wearing a T-shirt.
Grandfather has a cup of tea.
There are three mountains.
There is a fire beside the river.
The owl says, "Whoo-whoo!".
It's a very old car.
It's a happy face.
Rockets fly fast.

There are trees on the island.
Spencer and Click are in the boat with Ruth.
It is swimming in the ocean.
It has antlers.
It has stripes on its back and tail.
It's eating grain from the ground.
It has a big fluffy tail.
The fish is as big as the boat.
The boats aren't in the water.
The skeleton is made of <u>bones</u>.
His rock skipped three times.
They use their wings to fly.
Buzz puts the towel on his head.
He spits the water out of his mouth when he

He puts his hand over his nose.
They make a terrible smell when they are afraid.
She has her hand in her pocket.
He holds the cup and <u>saucer</u> in his hands.
The mountains are <u>covered</u> with snow.
The river is very cold.
The owl <u>calls</u>, "Whoo-whoo!" at night.
It has four wheels.
There's a <u>smile</u> on the face.
Fire comes from the back of the rocket.

It's an island in the ocean.	Ruth is rowing the boat.	It rhymes with sail.	It rhymes with hear.	It's sitting on a branch.
It's a chicken.	It's a squirrel.	Click caught an enormous fish.	The boats are on the sand.	Click found a fish skeleton.
Spencer can make rocks skip on the water.	The birds have wings.	BINGO	Buzz dries himself with a towel.	Ned got salt water in his mouth.
Ned smells something terrible.	Skunks are black and white animals.	Grandmother is wearing a T shirt.	Grandfather has a cup of tea.	There are three mountains.
There is a fire beside the river.	The owl says: "Whoo-whoo!"	It's a very old car.	It's a happy face.	Rockets fly fast.

There are trees on the island.	Spencer and Click are in the boat with Ruth.	It is swimming in the ocean.	It has antlers.	It has stripes on its back and tail.
It's eating grain from the ground.	It has a big fluffy tail.	The fish is as big as the boat.	The boats aren't in the water.	The skeleton is made of bones.
His rock skipped three times.	They use their wings to fly.	BINGO	Buzz puts the towel on his head.	He spits the salt water out of his mouth when he floats.
He puts his hand over his nose.	They make a terrible smell when they are afraid.	She has her hand in her pocket.	He holds the cup and saucer in his hands.	The mountains are covered with snow.
The river is very cold.	The owl calls: "Whoo-whoo!" at night.	It has four wheels.	There's a smile on the face.	Fire comes from the back of the rocket.

BOOK 3B   TEACHER'S GUIDE
BINGO 3   CARD 5

BOOK 3B   TEACHER'S GUIDE
BINGO 3   CARD 7

BOOK 3B   TEACHER'S GUIDE
BINGO 3   CARD 9

BOOK 3B   TEACHER'S GUIDE
BINGO 3   CARD 10

ANSWERS TO PAGE 81, LESSON 26 CROSSWORD PUZZLE

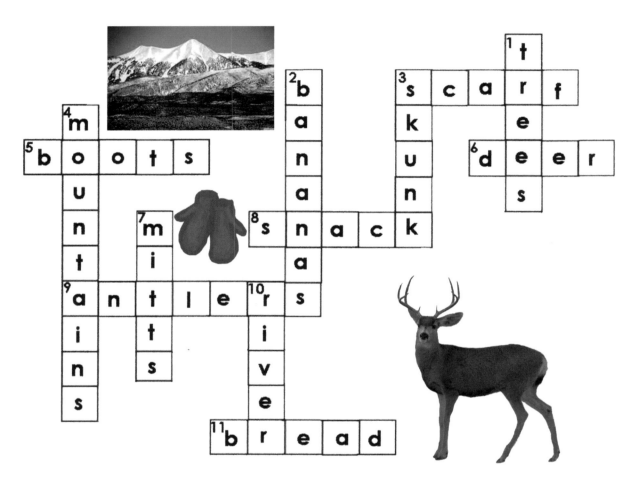

DOWN

1 ___Trees___ are in the forest.

2 ___Bananas___ are a fruit.

3 A ___skunk___ smells bad.

4 Some ___mountains___ are high.

7 ___Mitts___ keep your hands warm.

10 Water runs in the ___river___.

ACROSS

3 Spencer wore a ___scarf___.

5 You wear ___boots___ in the snow.

6 ___Deer___ live in the woods.

8 You eat a ___snack___.

9 Deer have ___antlers___.

11 The jay ate some ___bread___.

BOOK 3B   TEACHER'S GUIDE
PICTURE BINGO 4

For directions on how to play Picture Bingo go to Page 53 of this Guide.
These captions are also shown with their corresponding pictures on Pages 110 and 111.
Call them in a different order for each game.
The Enrichment Captions review the vocabulary that has been taught
and introduce some new words.
These words are underlined on this page only.

This Bingo Game reviews the vocabulary taught in Lessons 10 to 14.

BINGO 4 CAPTIONS

It rhymes with "float"'
Ruth is carrying a hat.
They are hiking boots.
There is a bear in the snow.
Their packsack is open.

The raccoon is a thief.
Click and Buzz are standing in the river.
Ruth is panning for gold.
This is a loaf of bread.
Buzz and Click are riding on the chairlift.
The moon and stars are bright.
This is the ski resort at night.
The skunk is making a terrible smell.
Nell got stuck in the snow.
Spencer skis very fast.
They are riding in the sleigh.
The eagle has a white head.
The jay is on the horse's back.
The snow is falling down.
The frog is sitting beside the river.
The fire makes smoke.
The friends are hiking.
The killer whales are near the beach.
The island is in the ocean.

BINGO 4 ENRICHMENT CAPTIONS

The boat is empty.
She is carrying her brother's hat.
They have long laces.
We can see the bear's footprints.
They have bread, bananas and honey for their snack.
This animal has a mask like a thief.
Click and Buzz are looking for gold in the river.
She hopes to find some gold.
We cut bread with a knife.
They are sitting on the chairlift seat.
They saw the moon behind a tree.
There is snow on the roof of the resort.
He put his hand over his nose.
Nell fell on her back in the snow.
He bends his knees when he skis.
Ruth is waving her hand from the sleigh.
It is sitting on top of a tree.
The horse has a white face.
It's snowing.
The frog has green spots.
The flames are red.
Ruth is leading the way.
Ruth is watching the killer whales.
The island is surrounded by water.

BOOK 3B
BINGO 4

TEACHER'S GUIDE
TEACHER'S COPY

It rhymes with "float".	Ruth is carrying a hat.	They are hiking boots.	There is a bear in the snow.	Their packsack is open.
The raccoon is a thief.	Click and Buzz are standing in the river.	Ruth is panning for gold.	This is a loaf of bread.	Buzz and Click are riding on the chairlift.
The moon and stars are bright.	This is the ski resort at night.	BINGO	The skunk is making a terrible smell.	Nell got stuck in the snow.
Spencer skis very fast.	They are riding in the sleigh.	The eagle has a white head.	The jay is on the horse's back.	The snow is falling down.
The frog is sitting beside the river.	The fire makes smoke.	The friends are hiking.	The killer whales are near the beach.	The island is in the ocean.

The boat is empty.

She is carrying her brother's hat.

They have long laces.

We can see the bear's footprints.

They have bread, bananas and honey for their snack.

This animal has a mask like a thief.

Click and Buzz are looking for gold in the river.

She hopes to find some gold.

We cut bread with a knife.

They are sitting on the chairlift seat.

They saw the moon behind a tree.

There is snow on the roof of the resort.

BINGO

He put his hand over his nose.

Nell fell on her back in the snow.

He bends his knees when he skis.

Ruth is waving her hand from the sleigh.

It is sitting on top of a tree.

The horse has a white face.

It's snowing.

The frog has green spots.

The flames are red.

Ruth is leading the way.

Ruth is watching the killer whales.

The island is surrounded by water.

BOOK 3B   TEACHER'S GUIDE
BINGO 4   CARD 1

BOOK 3B   TEACHER'S GUIDE
BINGO 4   CARD 6

BOOK 3B   TEACHER'S GUIDE
BINGO 4   CARD 7

BOOK 3B   TEACHER'S GUIDE
BINGO 4   CARD 8

BOOK 3B TEACHER'S GUIDE
BINGO 4 CARD 9

TEST: BOOK 3B   NAME: _____

To the teacher: Depending on the group you may wish to review the names of the pictures.
Test marks: Part1: 12 marks   Part 2:8 marks   Part 3: 5 marks

PART 1:   Print the missing letters.

1. ___ ___unks make a

terrible smell.

2. The mountains

have ___ ___ ow.

3. This is a ___ ___icken.

4. ___ ___uirrels eat

nuts.

5. This ro___ ___et is

flying to Saturn.

6. Click is

runn___ ___ ___.

7. Ned is learning to

___ ___ im.

8. This is a big

green ___ ___ee.

9. There are fi___ ___

In the ocean.

10. The Aliens live on

this ___ ___anet.

11. ___ ___abs

walk sideways.

12. Ned can

fl___ ___t.

i

Part 2:   **Read the question.**

Choose the correct answer from the box and print it on the line.

13. Can you swim?

_____

14. Do firecrackers go bang?

_____

15. Do fish live in trees?

_____

16. Do whales swim in the ocean?

_____

17. Is ocean water good to drink?

_____

18. Is it cold on a snowy mountain?

_____

19. Is it good to stand up in a small boat?

_____

20. Do you wear a toque on hot days?

_____

Yes, firecrackers go bang.   No, firecrackers don't go bang.

Yes, I can swim.   No, I can't swim.

Yes, whales swim in the ocean.   No, whales don't swim in the ocean.

Yes, fish live in trees.   No, fish don't live in trees.

Yes, I wear a toque on hot days.   No, I don't wear a toque on hot days.

Yes, it's good to stand up in a small boat.

No, it isn't good to stand up in a small boat.

Yes, it's cold on a snowy mountain.   No, it isn't cold on a snowy mountain.

Yes, ocean water is good to drink.   No, ocean water isn't good to drink.

PART 3:   Choose words from the box below to complete the sentences.

21. What has Click found?

Click has found a _____.

22. What is Nell holding?

Nell is holding a _____.

23. What is Ned doing?

Ned is trying to _____.

24. What is Ruth doing?

Ruth is _____.

25. What do you see on the rock?

I see the _____.

| fossil of a fish | skeleton | row | life preserver | skiing |

BOOK 3B   TEACHER'S GUIDE

ADVENTURES IN CANADA   GLOSSARY

A		Ee	
across		eagle	
address		eat (to) ate	
afraid		enormous	
after		explore (to) explored	
ahead		**F**	
along		fall (to), fell	
another		feet	
antler		fire	
anything		fish (to), fished	
B		flat	
backwards		feel (to) felt	
banana		flipper	
bathing suit		float (to), floated	
beach		fluffy	
behind		fly (to), flew	
below		food	
beside		footprint	
bigger than		forest	
bird		fossil	
boot		fresh	
bow (boat)		frighten (to), frightened	
branch		fruit	
bread		**G**	
bright		glad	
bump (to), bumped		gold	
C		grab (to), grabbed	
catch (to), caught		grain	
chairlift		grandfather	
chase (to) chased		grandmother	
		great	
chicken		ground	
chipmunk		**H**	
could		high	
crab		hike (to), hiked	
cup		hip hip hooray	
cut (to), cut		hold on (to), held on	
D		honey	
deer		hook (to), hooked	
dorsal fin		**I**	
drop (to), dropped		if	
drown (to), drowned		island	
dry (to), dried		**J**	
		jay	

K		Rr	
kick (to), kicked		rock	
kneel (to), kneeled		rod	
knife		row (to), rowed	
L		run away (to), ran away	
lake		**S**	
learn (to), learned		sail	
leaf - leaves		sand	
life preserver		saucer	
Mm		scarf	
mammal		seat	
matter		seed	
might		shoulder	
million		sideways	
mitt		skeleton	
monster		ski pole	
mountain		skip (to), skipped	
move (to), moved		skis	
must		skunk	
N		sleep (to) slept	
nice		sleeve	
night		sleigh	
nut		slide (to), slid	
Oo		slope	
oar		smell (to), smelt/smelled	
ocean		smoke (to), smoked	
P		smooth	
packsack		snack	
pair		snow	
piece		sock	
plate		some	
pocket		spit (to), spit	
pod of whales		squirrel	
point		stand up (to), stood up	
pour (to), poured		stern	
pull (to), pulled		stuck	
Qq		sunny	
R		swim (to), swam	
raccoon		**T**	
rain (to) rained		tea	
rent (to), rented		tell (to), told	
resort		tent	
ride (to), rode		terrible	
river		themselves	

BOOK 3B   TEACHER'S GUIDE

ADVENTURES IN CANADA   GLOSSARY

Tt		Ww	
there'll		wet	
tight		whale	
toque		what's	
towel		wheel	
trace (to), traced		whoo-whoo	
trail		window	
Uu		wing	
up		worry (to), worried	
Vv		would	
very		Xx	
W		Y	
warm		year	
watch (to), watched		Zz	

CPSIA information can be obtained at www.ICGtesting.com
Printed in the USA
LVIW01n0904140517
534481LV00008B/71